D0712704

# Ken Kutaragi

## PlayStation Developer

Other titles in the Innovators series include:

# INNOVATORS

# Ken Kutaragi

## *PlayStation Developer*

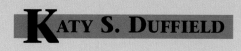

**K**ATY S. **D**UFFIELD

**KIDHAVEN PRESS**
*A part of Gale, Cengage Learning*

GALE
CENGAGE Learning™

Detroit • New York • San Francisco • New Haven, Conn • Waterville, Maine • London

© 2008 Gale, Cengage Learning

*For more information, contact*
KidHaven Press
27500 Drake Rd.
Farmington Hills, MI 48331-3535
Or you can visit our Internet site at gale.cengage.com

LIBRARY OF CONGRESS CATALOGING-IN-PUBLICATION DATA

Duffield, Katy S.
   Ken Kutaragi : PlayStation developer / by Katy S. Duffield.
      p. cm. — (Innovators)
   Includes bibliographical references and index.
   ISBN-13: 978-0-7377-3862-9 (hardcover)
   1. Kutaragi, Ken, 1950– 2. Computer engineers—Biography—Juvenile literature. 3. Sony
video games—History—Juvenile literature. I. Title.
   QA76.2.K984 2008
   621.39092—dc22
   [B]
                                                                  2007021913

ISBN-10: 0-7377-3862-6

Printed in the United States of America
 2 3 4 5 6 7 12 11 10 09 08

# CONTENTS

# A Creative Thinker

Ken Kutaragi is known as the father of PlayStation. Ever since he was a young man, Kutaragi carried with him the vision of a video game console that would have amazing sound combined with fast-paced, realistic computer **graphics**. Kutaragi's vision included remarkable high-tech ideas that would bring a new level of video game play directly into people's living rooms. With hard work and dedication, Kutaragi did just that—he invented one of the most successful and fastest-selling video game consoles in history.

The original PlayStation console was launched in the United States in 1995. Within six months, more than 1 million had been sold. And that was just the beginning. The phenomenal debut of the original PlayStation was followed up by Kutaragi's creation of PlayStation 2, PlayStation 3, and a handheld video game called PSP (PlayStation Portable). Upon the launch of each of these game units, thousands of people in Japan, the

**Ken Kutaragi invented the PlayStation, which became one of the most popular and profitable video game consoles in history.**

United States, and other countries camped out on storefront sidewalks and stood in long lines so they could be one of the first owners of Kutaragi's incredible machines.

Kutaragi has been called brash, talented, outspoken, and determined. But he is most often described as a visionary—a creative thinker who knows how to look into the future to develop **state-of-the-art** electronics that other engineers have not yet even considered.

# CHAPTER 1

# An Up-and-Coming Inventor

Ken Kutaragi was born in Tokyo, Japan, in 1950. His father, Takeji Kutaragi, was a businessman from the Japanese island of Kyushu who graduated from Taipei (Taiwan) University. For a time after college, Takeji owned a bookstore in Taipei. After World War II, however, he returned to Tokyo with his family and started a printing business. The family had little money during that time, but Takeji was not afraid of hard work. He was determined, with the help of his family, to make his new business a success.

## A Developing Work Ethic

Each day after school, young Ken pitched in at his father's printing shop. On most afternoons, he helped out in the workshop. He spent most evenings delivering goods to customers. On those long afternoons and evenings at the shop, Ken watched his father intently. He saw how hard his father worked to ensure the success of his business.

**Ken was born in Tokyo, Japan, in 1950. As a child, he helped in his father's printing business.**

As a boy, Ken sometimes worked late into the night delivering orders. He often did not return home until after 11:00 P.M. Even though he was often exhausted from these late hours, he did not neglect his schoolwork. He was a good student who made A's in all of his classes except physical education and social studies.

# Time for a Little Fun

Although Ken spent most of his time at school and at work, when he found a spare minute he went looking for a little fun. He loved tinkering with toys and mechanical things. Even at a young age, he had a strong curiosity and loved to figure out how things worked. When he was only ten years old, he had a friend who dreamed of being a rock star. To help out his buddy, Ken set to work on one of his first inventions. He created an amplifier that would help blast out the tunes from his friend's electric guitar.

**Even at a young age, Ken liked to invent. He invented an amplifier for his friend's guitar.**

Ken's inventions did not stop there. By the time he reached junior high, he became interested in cars, like many boys his age. He took apart old scooters and fashioned them into fast-moving go-carts. Throughout Ken's childhood, his parents noticed his interest in mechanics, and they never failed to encourage him. Whenever possible, they made sure he had opportunities to develop these skills while working at the print shop.

# College Life

After graduating from high school, Ken's love of invention and technology led him to apply to college at the University of Electro-Communications in Tokyo. The university offered classes in computer science, electronic and mechanical engineering, and hardware and computer **software** design. He was thrilled to have the chance to study subjects that fascinated him most.

Ken's course work increased his fascination with computer graphics, computer hardware, and computers in general. He wanted to learn everything he could about them. When he had the money, he bought computer-related gadgets so he could examine them. He once spent $1,000 on an electronic calculator—which was no small amount of money for him at that time. As Ken delved deeper into cutting-edge technology, he knew he wanted to spend his life pursuing these interests.

When Ken had to write an important paper to earn his college degree, he focused on how computer graphics could be used in various types of medical equipment. He did a lot of research and performed experiments to support the claims in his paper. When completed, his paper explained how computer graphics could be used to point out abnormalities in certain kinds of X-ray images.

During his college years Ken hoped to go into some type of engineering or electronics business, but when his father became ill, he reconsidered. He felt it was his duty to help keep the family business running. His father, however, had other ideas. He told his son, "You're an adult now, so from now on you must choose your own future. Don't feel obligated to stay in the family business."[1]

Ken took his father's words seriously. He asked himself, "What do I really like to do? What do I excel at? It has to be electronics and computers. If that were my work, every day would be a delight."[2] Ken was excited to have the opportunity to follow his dreams.

## Chasing Dreams

After graduating from college with an electrical engineering degree in 1975, Kutaragi had a decision to make. He thought for a while about starting his own business. He worried that it might be difficult to be successful fresh out of college, though. He thought he should gain some experience first, so he decided to begin his engineering career with an electronics company. Many of his fellow graduates were applying to Japan's public telephone company or one of many electrical equipment manufacturers, but these places did not interest him. As he focused on what he most enjoyed in life, he kept coming back to electronics and computers. Those areas, he decided, were where his future lay.

## A Home at Sony

In 1975 Kutaragi applied for an engineering job at the Sony Corporation, a company that developed and manufactured electronic items such as televisions, video cameras, stereos, and videocassette

Kutaragi knew his future career would involve electronics because of his passion for examining and taking apart electronics and computers, such as this computer motherboard.

**After college, Kutaragi accepted a position as an electrical engineer at the Sony Corporation.**

recorders. Even though most college graduates apply to several different companies to increase their chances of landing a job, Kutaragi applied only to Sony. He believed that Sony was the right place for him because, he said, "It was the best in terms of encouraging creativity and offering researchers freedom."[3]

Kutaragi also knew that Sony hired top engineers, and those engineers would be able to help him continue to learn and further his career. Even though Sony was hiring few new employees at the time, they saw potential in Kutaragi. He was offered a job as an electrical engineer.

# CHAPTER 2

# Challenges at Sony

Kutaragi went to work on several projects in Sony's First Development Division, where he quickly gained a reputation as a problem solver and a top-notch engineer. His focus and determination won him respect among fellow engineers and the company's upper-level management. But not all his early efforts met with success.

## Major Disappointment

Kutaragi's first project dealt with liquid crystal display (LCD) devices. LCDs are screens used to display numbers or images on electronic devices such as clocks, calculators, wristwatches, and CD players. During the 1970s, LCD displays were used only in calculators. Kutaragi's job was to find a way to apply LCD technology to television screens. Within a year after he arrived at Sony, his work led to a breakthrough on this assignment. He developed a model, called a **prototype,** of an LCD machine that would send out images and project them onto a large screen.

Kutaragi's first project dealt with liquid crystal display (LCD) devices, screens used to display numbers on electronic devices such as wristwatches.

Unfortunately for Kutaragi, his work on this project did not pay off. Other engineers within the company were working on similar types of projects using different kinds of technology. After company managers reviewed prototypes for all the projects, they did not choose Kutaragi's project for further development. Because Kutaragi had been with the company for only a short time, he had no control over his project's future. He was upset that he could not find a way to further it. He said, "I didn't have a hope. It was very disappointing."[4]

# A Step in the Right Direction

Despite the setback, Kutaragi was determined to succeed. Soon his persistence, hard work, and creativity gave him a chance to prove himself on a new project. Using some of the same methods he had developed in his LCD work, Kutaragi began to focus on light emitting diode (LED) technology. LEDs are the tiny many-colored lights that indicate whether an electronic item such as a computer monitor is off or on. They are also used as background lights in wristwatches, for television remote controls, and in some automobile dashboards.

Kutaragi thought about how he might apply LED technology to sound. During this time, most audio devices such as stereos used needle gauges to indicate volume level. Kutaragi experimented with LED lights to develop small graphs that would appear as lighted bars on the equipment to show volume.

When one of Sony's cofounders, Masaru Ibuka, visited the First Development Division, he looked over Kutaragi's shoulder as he worked. Ibuka was impressed with both Kutaragi and his project. He contacted Sony's Audio Division and told the managers there of Kutaragi's work. The LED bar graph display became Kutaragi's first successful project within the company. Its new design was not only useful, it looked flashy and modern too. This early achievement boosted Kutaragi's confidence and made him more determined than ever to continue inventing.

**Masaru Ibuka, one of Sony's cofounders, was so impressed by Kutaragi's work that he helped the younger man's newest project succeed.**

# Ahead of His Time

In the early 1980s Kutaragi began a major project centered on a computer storage device called a floppy disk, or diskette. These devices were intended to store and transport computer files. Two separate engineering teams at Sony were assigned to work on different types of diskettes. Kutaragi and his team worked on a 2-inch diskette (5.08cm), while the other team developed a 3.5-inch version (8.89cm). The teams competed against one another, and each hoped that Sony management would adopt its version.

As the time approached for management to make a decision, Kutaragi and his team worked overtime to develop their prototype. When the decision was finally made, both teams

**In the early 1980s two teams at Sony, one led by Kutaragi, developed separate versions of floppy disks, or diskettes.**

were winners. The 3.5-inch diskette (8.89cm) was chosen to be used in computers, while Kutaragi's 2-inch version (5.08cm) would have a different use. At this time, **digital** cameras had not yet been invented, so people still took photographs using film that had to be developed. Kutaragi's floppy disk provided a way for photographic images to be stored without film, and Sony created an early digital camera. This accomplishment proved again that Kutaragi was a determined and valuable member of the company.

# Digital Technology: A New Beginning

At the time Kutaragi was working on the floppy disk project, digital technology was still fairly new. Personal computers for home use were only beginning to gain popularity. This new technology excited Kutaragi. As soon as all the necessary parts were available, he purchased everything he needed to build his own personal computer from scratch. He was not about to be left behind—and he did not want to see Sony left behind either. Kutaragi said, "My role is to help lead the company into the future."[5] He had no doubt that digital technology was the key to that future.

As an inventor, Kutaragi saw unlimited possibilities with the use of digital technology. According to writer Kenneth Li, Kutaragi wanted to transform the work at Sony "from the analog world of radios, recorders, and TVs to the digital world of compact discs and computers."[6] Unfortunately for Kutaragi, managers at Sony wanted to conduct business the way they always had. They were not sure that venturing into the new digital age was a good idea. So whenever Kutaragi suggested that the company head in a more digitally oriented direction, he was disregarded. In fact, when an older coworker heard that Kutaragi was pushing for more digital projects, he told Kutaragi, "You must never say that at Sony. You'll be transferred immediately."[7]

Disappointed, Kutaragi felt his creativity had been blocked. But then he discovered a division of Sony he had not known existed—a digital research center. He immediately requested a transfer to the center and was delighted when it was approved. In his new surroundings, Kutaragi and a number of other young digital engineers were able to feed their passion for digital technology.

## A Partner in Nintendo

Around the time of his transfer, Kutaragi bought a video game console that had recently been released by Nintendo, another electronics company. Known as the Nintendo Entertainment System, or NES, the machine had rapidly gained popularity and was the fastest-selling game console of its time. After playing and testing the game, Kutaragi took the console apart piece by piece to see how it worked. He studied each component of the machine to see if he could figure out how to make it better.

**Kutaragi wanted Sony to move into the new digital world of computers and compact discs.**

**After playing and testing the Nintendo Entertainment System, a video game console made by another electronics company, Kutaragi knew he wanted to develop similar products at Sony.**

A few years later, Nintendo engineers contacted Kutaragi to see if Sony would be interested in becoming partners to develop a **sound chip.** The sound chip in a video game is what gives it a clear, realistic sound. Because Kutaragi was interested in all phases of game console development, he immediately agreed to work with Nintendo. This was his chance to learn more about the business and perhaps interest Sony in delving deeper into the game console market. Kutaragi worked on the project in 1986 and 1987, and it turned out to be a success.

# CHAPTER 3

# The PlayStation Phenomenon

After Sony and Nintendo worked together on the sound chip, Kutaragi was thrilled when the two groups decided to partner on a brand-new game console. Kutaragi could not wait to get started on the project. He and his team set out to develop what he hoped would become the greatest video game console ever invented. In 1991, however, just as the project began, Nintendo officials pulled out of the agreement and went into partnership with another company. Kutaragi was upset and disappointed, but he refused to quit. He had made up his mind that Sony should find a place in the emerging video game market —but first he had to convince the company's managers.

Sony executives were not enthusiastic about Kutaragi's ideas about entering the game market. They looked down on video games as mere toys. They saw Sony as an important electronics company with a strong reputation in high-end electronics. They wanted to stay with what they knew rather than move into a new and unfamiliar market. Kutaragi was frustrated by this attitude. At one point he threatened to quit if he were not allowed to pursue the project. He recalled, "I was very sad. But I had a strong passion to make my vision a reality, even if that meant leaving Sony."[8]

## The Go-Ahead

Kutaragi felt so strongly about designing and developing a video game console for Sony that one day he boldly marched into the office of Norio Ogha, a high-ranking executive. Kutaragi told Ogha that he and his team had been secretly working on a new

**Kutaragi (pictured in 2003) wanted Sony to enter the video game market.**

**Kutaragi wanted to develop a new, more realistic and thrilling video game console that used three-dimensional graphics.**

game console that, unlike any other consoles on the market, used **three-dimensional (3-D)** technology. Kutaragi explained that this technology would make the game effects much more realistic and thrilling. Instead of looking flat on the screen, the images would appear rounded and true to life. Kutaragi excitedly outlined his vision for the project and awaited Ogha's answer.

Kutaragi's enthusiasm, along with Ogha's own anger over being rejected by Nintendo, convinced Ogha. Kutaragi said, "Mr. Ogha responded with energy, saying . . . [to] show him the proof that I could do it. Then he boiled over, clenching his fists and bellowing, 'Do it!'"[9] Ogha had such faith in Kutaragi's ideas and his abilities as an engineer that he put Kutaragi in charge of the project.

## PlayStation Lives!

Kutaragi and his team immediately plunged into work on the PS/X, the code name for the video game console. Kutaragi recalled a stunning 3-D computer graphics system called System G that he had first learned about a few years earlier. The G in System G stands for the Japanese word *gaza,* which means "image." The images System G produced looked more realistic than anything Kutaragi had ever seen on a computer screen. Also, the images could instantly be moved around on the screen with the simple touch of a slide control. Kutaragi said, "It was awesome. I was really impressed that such a thing existed."[10] Kutaragi knew this was the type of technology he wanted to use to make Sony's game console unlike any other.

It took Kutaragi and his team about three years to complete the project, which was eventually named PlayStation. Kutaragi explained how the game console got its name: "If a computer for work is a workstation, a computer for play is a 'playstation.'"[11]

Kutaragi concentrated on making every part of the console the best it could be. Unlike many types of electronics, PlayStation was not made using parts, called **components**, designed and built by other companies. Instead, Kutaragi and his team built every piece of the machine from scratch. He was so passionate about each detail of his work that he was even said to have challenged a coworker to an arm wrestling match to settle a dispute over the game console's design.

When prototypes of the first PlayStation were completed, Kutaragi and his team delivered what they had promised. The unit's 3-D graphics, sparkling sound, and quick-responding controllers were superior to anything Sony executives had ever seen before. Managers were so pleased with Kutaragi's work on the PlayStation that they named him Director and General Manager of Sony's Research and Development Division in 1993.

Kutaragi and his team made final changes and adjustments on the game machine. When everything was just as they wanted it, the unit went into production. As thousands of consoles rolled off the assembly line, Sony's advertising department began a marketing campaign to introduce the PlayStation, first to Japan and then to the world.

## The Launch

On December 2, 1994, the night before the PlayStation game console was to go on sale in Japan, Kutaragi was nervous. He knew he and his team had developed an exciting new product, but until the console went on sale, no one could predict just how successful it would be.

**Kutaragi and his team created and built every part of PlayStation from scratch.**

The next morning, Kutaragi pulled on a PlayStation sweatshirt and headed downtown to a local business where the console would be sold. Much to his surprise and joy, a line of several hundred people stretched down the street in front of the store. Reports of long lines came in from other areas of the city as well. Storeowners told of people camping out overnight to be among the first in line to purchase one of the new game consoles. By noon, almost every single PlayStation console available

**29**

for sale in Japan had been sold. Before the day was through, 100,000 units had been purchased.

Kutaragi, his team, and Sony managers were excited about the sales success in Japan. But the achievement caused some unforeseen problems as well. The group had hoped the PlayStation would be successful; but they never expected that it would

**People camped out overnight to be among the first in line to purchase one of the new PlayStations.**

become such a sensation. The production team had manufactured only 300,000 consoles, so they had to get back to work to increase production in order to meet the demand. With the North American launch only a few months away, production of the console was hurried so there would be plenty of machines available for sale.

In 1995 the PlayStation made its first appearance in the United States. As in Japan, the console was an immediate hit. Over 100,000 units sold in the first weekend alone. Players could not wait to try out games such as *Ridge Racer, Final Fantasy,* and *Grand Turismo.* The popularity of these games helped PlayStation become one of the fastest-selling video game consoles of its time. Although Kutaragi was overjoyed with his accomplishment, he did not intend to simply relax and enjoy it. He already had even bigger and better things in mind.

# CHAPTER 4

# The Phenomenon Continues

The launch of the first PlayStation console was only the beginning for Kutaragi. Before the console had even been released, he was already making plans for what would come next. He said, "I am an engineer and I like technology. I want to change the world with technology and I want to change our lives. The best way to realize it is, for us, PlayStation."[12]

## PlayStation 2

Sony executives may have been unsure at first about entering the video game console market, but the overwhelming success of the first PlayStation convinced them to spend $2.5 billion for Kutaragi to create the PlayStation 2. Shortly after the release of the original PlayStation, Kutaragi and his team went back to work to develop an even more advanced game machine.

As with the first PlayStation, Kutaragi and his team assembled the entire unit from scratch. For this version, Kutaragi introduced a new type of **central processing unit (CPU).** A CPU

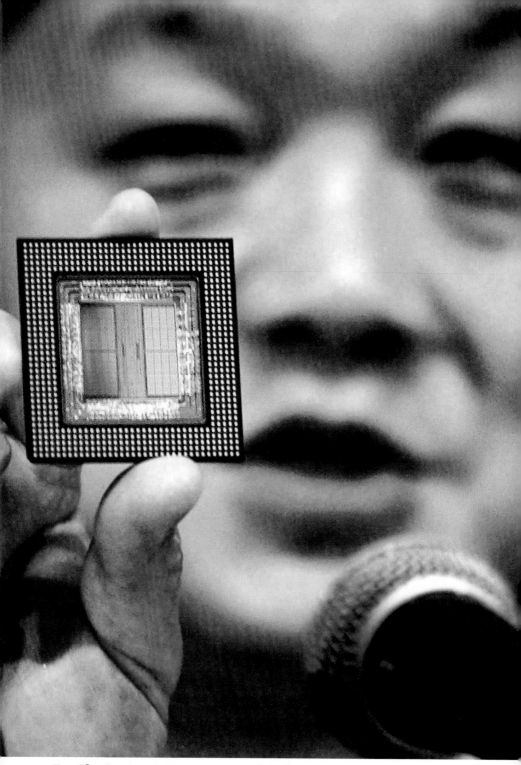

For PlayStation 2, Kutaragi introduced a new type of central processing unit (CPU), which he named the Emotion Engine.

In 2005 Kutaragi released the PlayStation Portable (PSP), which allowed gamers to play wherever and whenever they liked.

is the part of a game console or computer that carries out the instructions of the computer game or program. Kutaragi called his CPU the Emotion Engine. It was capable of even more amazingly realistic graphics than the original PlayStation. In the original PlayStation, the building blocks of the processor used to create 3-D graphics moved at a pace of 360,000 per second, while the Emotion Engine's building blocks moved at 20 million per second. To go along with the new graphics, Kutaragi and his team added a DVD player and Internet capability.

In 2000, about five years after the launch of the original PlayStation, the PlayStation 2 was released. In Japan alone, almost 1 million machines were purchased. Upon its U.S. release, the PlayStation 2 was said to have been the fastest-selling video game console at launch. Kutaragi and his team had done it again.

## PSP—PlayStation Portable

For his next project, Kutaragi continued to concentrate on video games, but this time he and his team began work on the PSP, or PlayStation Portable. Kutaragi called this handheld video game unit the "new baby in the family."[13] His team had to move quickly to meet deadlines, but they succeeded. By 2005 the new game system had been completed.

With the introduction of the PSP, serious gamers no longer had to leave their favorite games behind—they could take them along wherever they went. And the PSP was not simply just a game system. Owners could watch movies, listen to their favorite music, and even view photos on their new systems. Since the PSP can wirelessly connect to the Internet, a user might do a little Web surfing or play a head-to-head game of *Ratchet and*

*Clank* with a friend across the country. Kutaragi said, "We introduced this product to change the world. A portable system for everyone."[14]

Kutaragi's hard work, vision, and dedication to the PlayStation projects eventually earned him notice outside the video game world. In 2002 he was named one of *BusinessWeek* magazine's "Best Managers," and in 2004 *Time* magazine included him on their list of the 100 Most Influential People of the year. Kutaragi had accomplished a lot since his first days at Sony, but he was not finished yet.

# PlayStation 3

Kutaragi's next venture would be continuing to make the PlayStation video game console faster, better, and even more realistic. According to the project manager, Kutaragi "wanted to go 1,000 times more realistic than PlayStation 2."[15] To do that, Kutaragi and his team developed a superfast central processing unit called the Cell. Sources say Kutaragi put together a team of about 400 engineers from three different companies and spent nearly $400 million to develop the processor. Along with the exciting new processor, Kutaragi added a wireless controller and a state-of-the-art DVD player called Blu-ray.

Like the original PlayStation and the PlayStation 2, the PlayStation 3 was eagerly awaited by tens of thousands of gaming fans throughout the world. It was supposed to go on sale in early 2006, but was delayed by component shortages and production problems. Finally, in November 2006 gamers got their first glimpse of the new machine. Again, thousands of people camped out in front of stores and stood in line for hours to be able to purchase one of the consoles.

Sales numbers showed that the PlayStation 3 was a success. Six months after its launch, 1 million PlayStation 3 consoles had been shipped in North America. It also won many awards, including an Emmy Award for technology and engineering, the CES Best of Innovations Award for 2007, and *PC World*'s 20 Most Innovative Products Award.

**This young man waited in line overnight to purchase a PlayStation 3 immediately after it was released.**

# The Future

Kutaragi has always been known as a visionary, a man who has the ability to think ahead. Even after all he has accomplished with PlayStation, his dreams are not yet complete. He is already planning a PlayStation 4. And he has entered into an agreement with a software manufacturing company. The new company, called Cellius, plans to develop a line of video games that will

**Kutaragi has many plans for his future at Sony, including developing PlayStation 4 and enhancing the video games for it.**

work with PlayStation 3's Cell processor. Kutaragi will apply his knowledge and experience in this new area to take games like *Need for Speed, Sonic the Hedgehog, MLB*, and many others to new levels.

Concerning the future, Kutaragi said, "I am really pleased to be occasionally called the father of the PlayStation. But my dream, and the dream of all my team, hasn't finished. In fact we haven't achieved even half of what we're going to do."[16]

# NOTES

## Chapter 1: An Up-and-Coming Inventor

1. Quoted in Reiji Asakura, *Revolutionaries at Sony*. New York: McGraw-Hill, 2000, p. 7.
2. Quoted in Asakura, *Revolutionaries at Sony*, p. 8.
3. Quoted in *BusinessWeek Online*, "Ken Kutaragi: Is Sony's Future in His Hands?" *BusinessWeek Online*, June 14, 1999. www.businessweek.com/1999/99_24/b3633067.htm?script Framed.

## Chapter 2: Challenges at Sony

4. Quoted in Asakura, *Revolutionaries at Sony*, p. 10.
5. Quoted in Jim Frederick, "Playing His Way to the Next Level," *Time*, December 1, 2003, p. 84.
6. Kenneth Li, "Meet the Man Behind Sony's PlayStation," CNN.com, September 1, 2000. http://archives.cnn.com/2000/TECH/computing/09/01/meet.ken.kutaragi.idg/index.html.
7. Quoted in Asakura, *Revolutionaries at Sony*, p. 17.

## Chapter 3: The PlayStation Phenomenon

8. Quoted in Adam Morgan, *The Pirate Inside: Building a Challenger Brand Culture within Yourself and Your Organization*. New Jersey: John Wiley and Sons, 2004, p. 126.
9. Quoted in Mike Dolan, "Behind the Screens," *Wired News*, May 2001. www.wired.com/wired/archive/9.05/history_pr. html.

10. Quoted in Asakura, *Revolutionaries at Sony.* p. 3.

11. Quoted in Asakura, *Revolutionaries at Sony,* p. 30.

## Chapter 4: The Phenomenon Continues

12. Quoted in Richard Taylor, "Nurturing the PlayStation Dream," BBC News, BBC Click Online, November 11, 2005. http://newsvote.bbc.co.uk/mpapps/pagetools/print/news.bbc. co.uk/2/hi/programmes/click_online/4428626.stm.

13. Quoted in Tom Mainelli, "Sony's PlayStation Goes Portable," *PC World.com,* May, 13, 2003. http://pcworldabout.com/news/May132003id110722.htm.

14. Quoted in Steven Levy, "Sony Gets Personal," *Newsweek,* November 1, 2004, pp. 50–57.

15. Quoted in David Kirkpatrick, "The 9-in-1 Wonder Chip," *Fortune,* September 5, 2005, pp. 139–40.

16. Quoted in Taylor. "Nurturing the PlayStation Dream."

# GLOSSARY

**central processing unit (CPU):** The part of a computer that carries out the instructions of the computer game or program.

**components:** The different parts that make up an electronic device.

**digital:** Certain devices such as computers that can read, write, and store information that is written as a series of 0's and 1's.

**graphics:** Pictures generated on a computer screen.

**prototype:** A working model of a product that enables engineers and others to test the design and see what the finished product will look like.

**software:** Computer programs that control how a computer works.

**sound chip:** A device that gives video games and other electronic devices a clear, realistic sound.

**state-of-the-art:** Describes something that uses the newest and most advanced technology.

**three-dimensional (3-D):** Describes images that look more rounded and realistic than pictures on a flat screen normally appear.

# FOR FURTHER EXPLORATION

## Books

Jan Burns, *Innovators: Shigeru Miyamoto*. Detroit, MI: Kid-Haven, 2006. This book tells about the man who invented some of the world's most famous video games. Readers will learn more about the game designer who created such groundbreaking games as *Donkey Kong, The Legend of Zelda*, and *Super Mario Bros.*

Rusel DeMaria and Johnny Wilson, *High Score! The Illustrated History of Electronic Games*. 2nd ed. New York: McGraw-Hill, Osborne Media, 2003. This highly illustrated book covers 30 years of video game history including information on the most popular arcades, consoles, and games.

Catherine Thimmesh, *Girls Think of Everything: Stories of Ingenious Inventions by Women*. New York: Houghton Mifflin, 2000. This book tells about the women who invented windshield wipers, space bumpers that protect spacecraft, paper that allows people to write in the dark, and many other inventions.

## Web Sites

**Game Machines.com** (www.game-machines.com). Visit this site to find information on every type of game console ever produced. The site also includes up-to-date news on consoles and games.

**How Stuff Works** (www.howstuffworks.com/video-game.htm). This site gives a fascinating inside look at how PlayStation and other game consoles, controllers, and games work.

**The Official PlayStation Website** (www.us.playstation.com). This site contains information about the PlayStation 2 and 3 consoles and the PlayStation Portable (PSP). It also offers PlayStation news, games, and support.

# INDEX

# PICTURE CREDITS

# About the Author

Katy S. Duffield has been writing for children and young adults for more than ten years. Her books include a picture book for young readers, *Farmer McPeepers and His Missing Milk Cows*, and a nonfiction book for older readers, *Mysterious Encounters: Poltergeists*. Duffield's work has also appeared in many magazines, including *Highlights for Children, Family Fun, AppleSeeds, Guideposts for Kids, Focus on the Family Clubhouse*, and many others. Her Web site is www.katyduffield.com.